Paw Prints

Great Danes

by Nadia Higgins

Ideas for Parents and Teachers

Bullfrog Books let children practice reading informational text at the earliest reading levels. Repetition, familiar words, and photo labels support early readers.

Before Reading

- Discuss the cover photo. What does it tell them?

- Look at the picture glossary together. Read and discuss the words.

Read the Book

- "Walk" through the book and look at the photos. Let the child ask questions. Point out the photo labels.

- Read the book to the child, or have him or her read independently.

After Reading

- Prompt the child to think more. Ask: Have you ever seen a Great Dane? Would you like to play with one?

Bullfrog Books are published by Jump!
5357 Penn Avenue South
Minneapolis, MN 55419
www.jumplibrary.com

Library of Congress Cataloging-in-Publication Data

Names: Higgins, Nadia, author.
Title: Great Danes / by Nadia Higgins.
Description: Minneapolis, MN : Jump!, Inc., 2018.
Series: Paw prints | Series: Bullfrog books
Includes index.
Audience: Ages 5 to 8. | Audience: Grades K to 3.
Identifiers: LCCN 2017042559 (print)
LCCN 2017044188 (ebook)
ISBN 9781624967771 (ebook)
ISBN 9781624967764 (hardcover : alk. paper)
Subjects: LCSH: Great Dane—Juvenile literature.
Classification: LCC SF429.G7 (ebook)
LCC SF429.G7 H54 2018 (print) | DDC 636.73—dc23
LC record available at https://lccn.loc.gov/2017042559

Editor: Jenna Trnka
Book Designer: Molly Ballanger

Photo Credits: Lindsay Helms/Shutterstock, cover; Eric Isselee/Shutterstock, 1, 3, 22; Newspix/Getty, 4; Tierfotoagentur/Alamy, 5; Grisha Bruev/Shutterstock, 6–7; Sharon Vos-Arnold/Getty, 8–9; DragoNika/Shutterstock, 10–11, 23tl; Jean Michel Labat/Pantheon/SuperStock, 12–13; ChristopherBernard/iStock, 14–15, 23bl; Erik Lam/Shutterstock, 16, 24; Erich Schmidt/imageBROKER/SuperStock, 17; Elizabeth Whiting & Associates/Alamy, 18–19; Roger costa morera/Shutterstock, 20–21, 23br; iustsolove/Shutterstock, 23tr.

Printed in the United States of America at Corporate Graphics in North Mankato, Minnesota.

Table of Contents

Gentle Giants 4

A Great Dane Up Close 22

Picture Glossary 23

Index 24

To Learn More 24

Gentle Giants

What is that
huge dog?

It is a Great Dane!

5

Woof!

Its bark is loud.

Don't be scared.

This dog is sweet.

It is a gentle giant.

Great Danes were
bred in Germany.

They were hunters.

This dog is very strong.
It can run fast.

Look at its long legs.

coat

Pet it.

Feel its smooth coat.

These dogs come in lots of colors.
Yellow, black, white, and gray.
Some have spots.

Some have stripes.

These dogs are huge.
This one takes up
the whole sofa!

Nudge, nudge.

This one pushes
with her head.

What does she want?

More petting, please!

A Great Dane Up Close

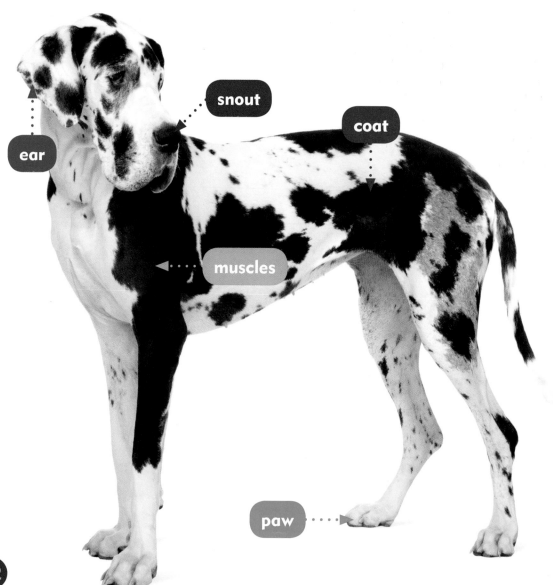

ear

snout

coat

muscles

paw

Picture Glossary

bred
Developed as
a dog breed.

Germany
A country
in Western
Europe.

coat
A dog's fur.

nudge
To push gently.

Index

bark 6

coat 15

colors 16

gentle 9

Germany 10

huge 4, 19

hunters 10

legs 13

nudge 20

stripes 17

strong 12

sweet 9

To Learn More

Learning more is as easy as 1, 2, 3.

1) Go to www.factsurfer.com

2) Enter "greatdanes" into the search box.

3) Click the "Surf" button to see a list of websites.

With factsurfer.com, finding more information is just a click away.